Multiplying and dividing

Paul Harling

Contents

Page		
2	Frying tonight	Code puzzle
3	Facts about 72	Mixed multiplying and dividing
4	Games squares	Games on a hundred square
5	Dodges with digits	Calculator number patterns • Problem
6	Factors and multiples	Factors and multiples on a graph
7	Five in a line	Tables game
8	Back to brackets	Using brackets • Problem
9	Precision division	Rules for dividing by 3, 9 and 4
10	Russian multiplication	Doubling and halving
11	Doubles and trebles Cross – number	Number problems
12	Lattice multiplication	Other ways to multiply
13	Napier's bones	Other ways to multiply
14	Four rules! Eleven divides!	Using the four rules of number
15	Dotty crosses	Number pattern investigations • Problem
16	Prime numbers	Eratosthenes' sieve
17	More about prime numbers	Goldbach's conjecture
18	Number power	Introducing and using index notation
20	What is a million?	Investigating one million
21	On the trillion trail Super dividends	Investigation • Super dividends
22	Getting it taped	Problem solving • Puzzle
23	Fair shares?	Problem solving
24	When will they meet again?	Problem solving

Frying tonight

What plays the bagpipes while cooking chips?

Work with a friend. Find the answer to this question by working out the calculations below.
Each result stands for a letter of the alphabet.
Write the letters in order and the question will be answered.

A	C	E	F	G	H	I	M	N	O	R	S	T	Y
37	289	8	42	33	121	729	0	2	3	32	712	63	40

9	11	64
× 7	× 11	÷ 8
= 63	= □	= □
T	?	?

There are quick ways to do some of the calculations.
For example, multiplying by 10 and then dividing by 5 is the same as multiplying by 2.

21	16	1000	9	780	99
× 10	× 16	÷ 25	× 9	÷ 5	× 5
÷ 5	÷ 8		× 9	÷ 78	÷ 15
= □	= □	= □	= □	= □	= □
?	?	?	?	?	?

89	17	189	315	178	500	111	512
× 8	× 17	÷ 63	÷ 5	× 4	× 6	× 111	÷ 256
			÷ 1		× 0	÷ 333	
= □	= □	= □	= □	= □	= □	= □	= □
?	?	?	?	?	?	?	?

Make up another puzzle like this for your friend to answer.

Facts about 72

1 Copy this and fill in the missing numbers.

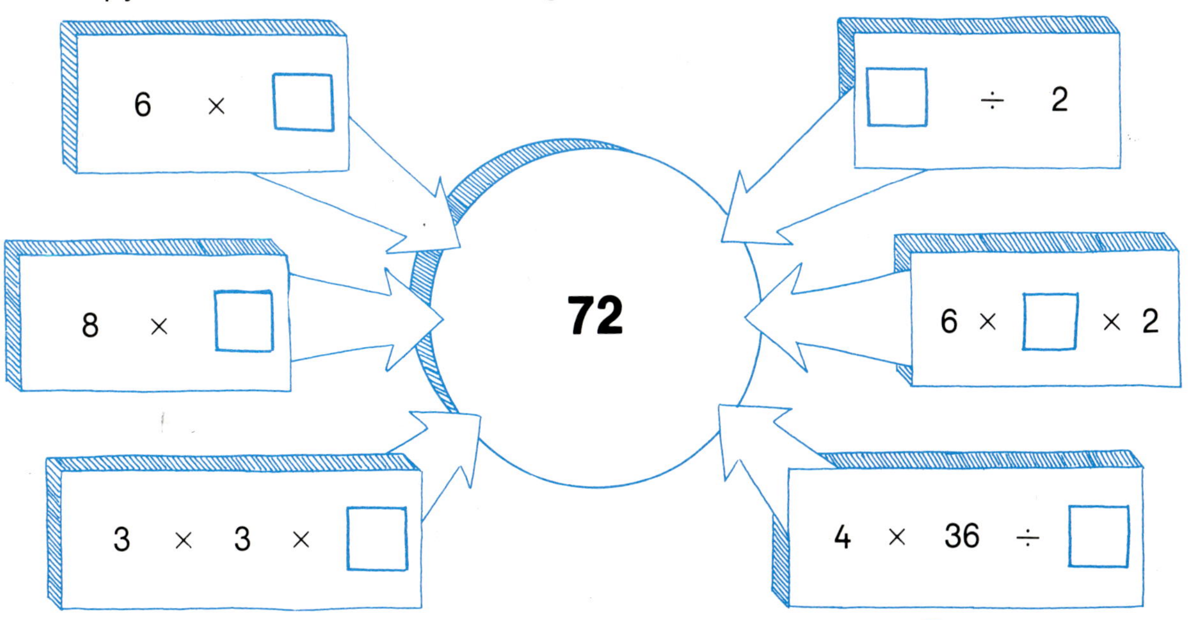

2 Work with a friend. Use each of these ways to make 72. Write each calculation down.

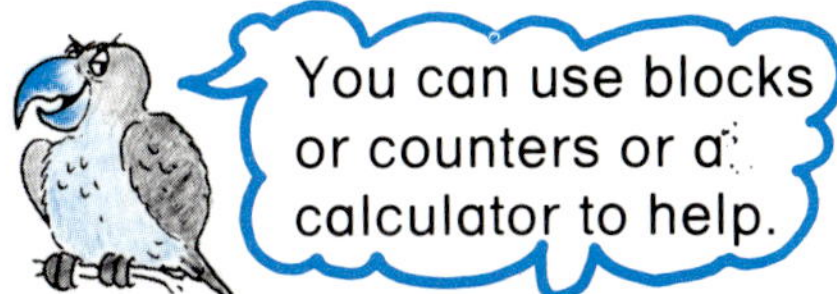

Make 72 by multiplying	Make 72 by dividing
a Multiply two different numbers that are between 6 and 10. **b** Multiply two numbers. One of them is equal to 6 × 2. **c** Multiply three numbers. Two of them are 9 and 4. **d** Multiply three numbers. Two of them are the same and the other is 2. **e** Multiply three numbers. One of them is 12. The other two are less than 5.	For these you need to think of two numbers, one smaller than the other. Divide the larger by the smaller. **a** The larger number is 144. **b** The smaller number is 3. **c** The larger number is 288. **d** The larger number is 720. **e** A three-digit number and a one-digit number.

3 Ask your friend to choose another number. In five minutes, which of you can find most ways to make this number?

Games squares

Play these games with a friend.
You need a large hundred square,
two dice, and a counter each.

Sixes and sevens

1 Throw two dice.

2 Move forward the number of places shown by the score on the dice.

3 If it is a **multiple of 6** move on 4 more places.

4 If it is a **multiple of 7** move back 8 places.

5 First to pass 100 is the winner.

Watch out for numbers which are multiples of 6 **and** 7 – then you have to move **both** ways!

Lucky triangles

1 Throw one die.

2 Move forward the number of places shown by the score on the die.

3 If you land on a **triangular** number, move on to the next **triangular** number.

4 If you land on a **square** number, move back to the previous **square** number.

5 36 and 1 are both square **and** triangular numbers. If you land on 1, start again. If you land on 36 go straight to 100!

6 You need an exact score to reach 100. You cannot overrun.

Remember:
Triangular numbers can be pictured as triangles.

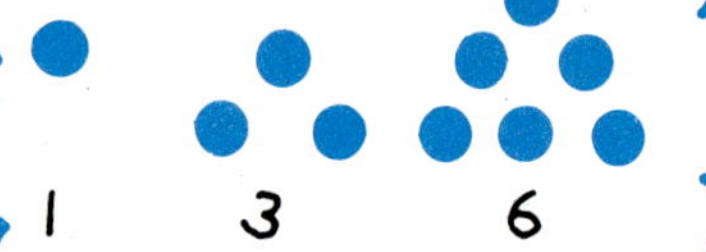

Square numbers can be pictured as squares.

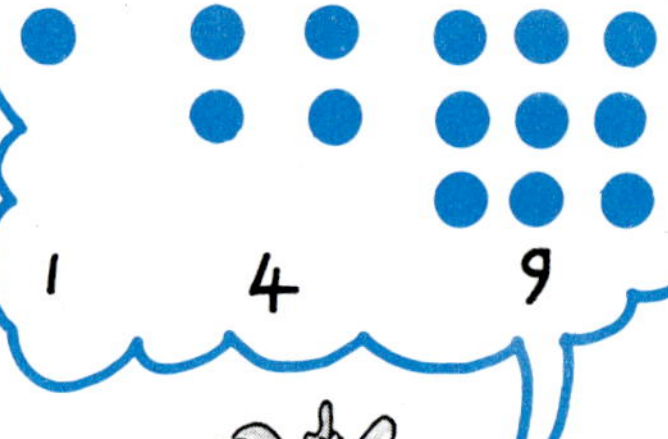

Make up another game like this with your friend.
Write down the rules so other people can play it.

Dodges with digits

1 Write these down and work them out using a calculator.

a 41 × 35 = ☐ **b** 15 × 93 = ☐ **c** 351 × 9 = ☐
d 81 × 27 = ☐ **e** 21 × 87 = ☐ **f** 8 × 473 = ☐

What do you notice about the digits in each question and its answer?

18 × 297 = 5346
In this calculation, each of the digits 1, 2, 3, 4, 5, 6, 7, 8 and 9 is used only once.

2 Do the calculations below work in the same way?
When you have found each answer, check it using a calculator.

a 1738 × 4

b 1963 × 4

c 483 × 12

d 12) 5796

e 42) 5796

f 198 × 27

g 186 × 39

h 159 × 48

i 28) 4396

Puzzler

The bike shop has a special offer. If you buy a new bike, you can choose **three** free 'extras' with it.
You can choose from this list:

Write down all the **different** sets of three extras you could choose.

Factors and multiples

On the grid below the factors of 24 have been marked with crosses.

1 Work with a friend. Copy the grid on to squared paper.

Decide which axis shows the **factors**. Label it.
Label the other axis for the **multiples**.

Complete the grid by marking in the factors for all the numbers up to 23.

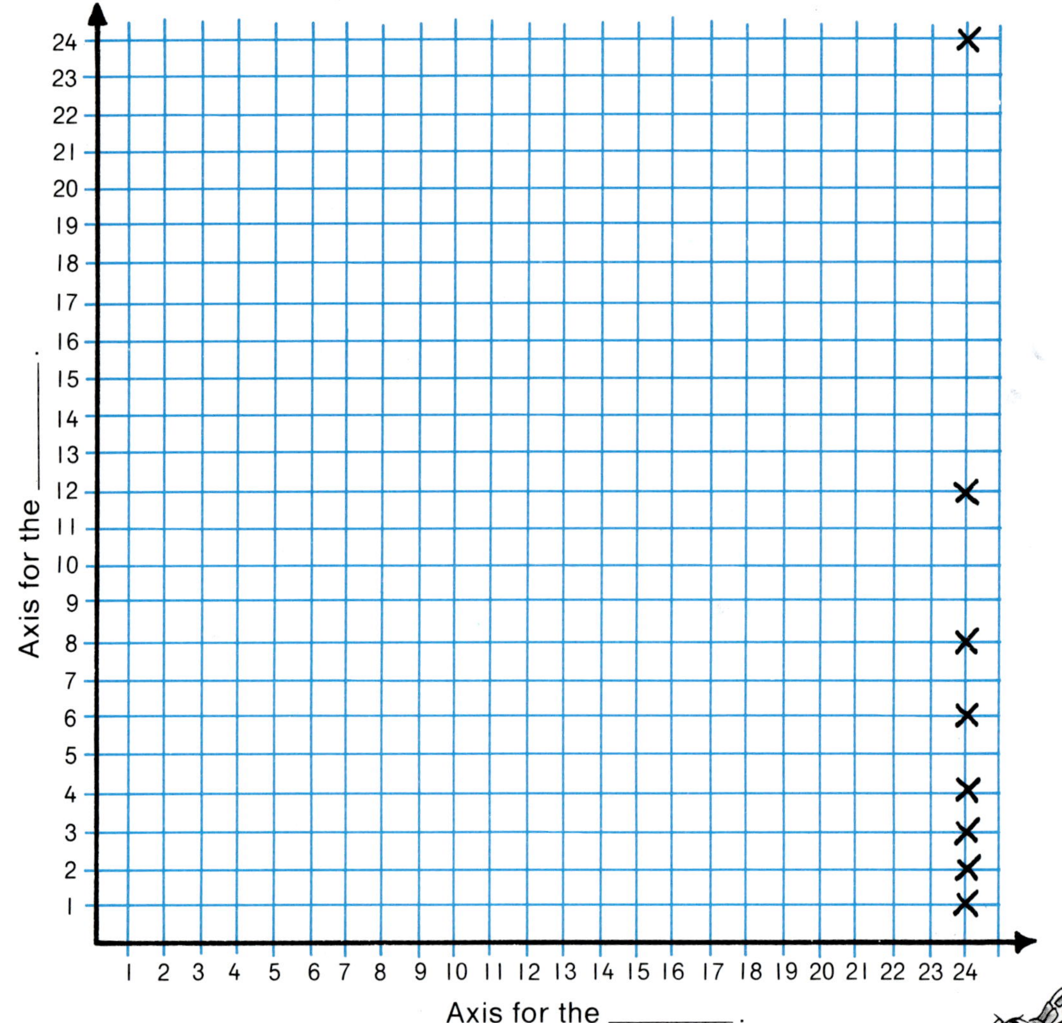

2 Write about any interesting patterns you find.

Five in a line

Play this game with a friend. You need a multiplication square, two dice, and a pen or pencil each of a different colour.

Take turns to throw the two dice.
If you score 4, you can circle
ONE multiple of 4 on the square.
So you can circle either
4, 8, 12, 16, 20, 24, 28, 32, 36, 40, 48, 56, 60, 64, 72, 80 or 100.

If your friend scores 9, he or she
can circle **ONE multiple** of 9.
9, 18, 27, 36, 45, 54, 63, 72, 81 or 90.

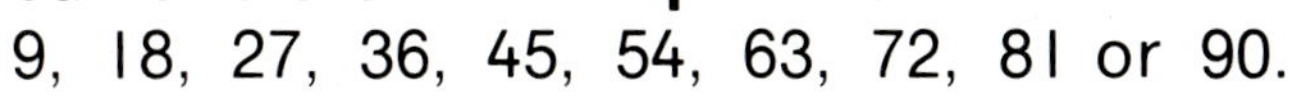

The same rule is used for other scores.

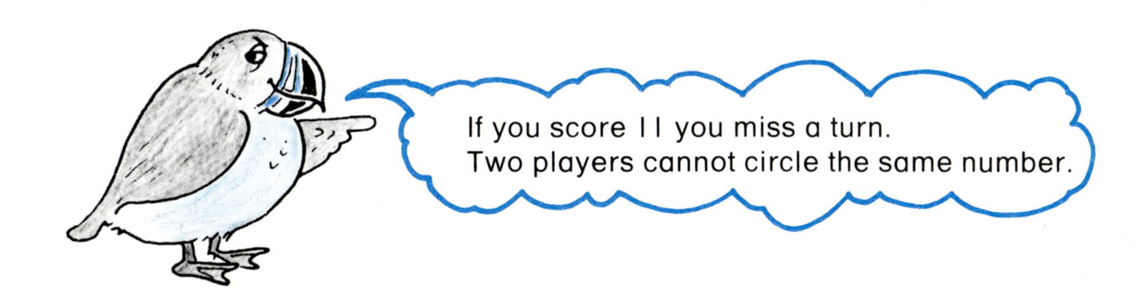

The winner is the first to circle **five numbers** in a column

or in a row

or in a diagonal.

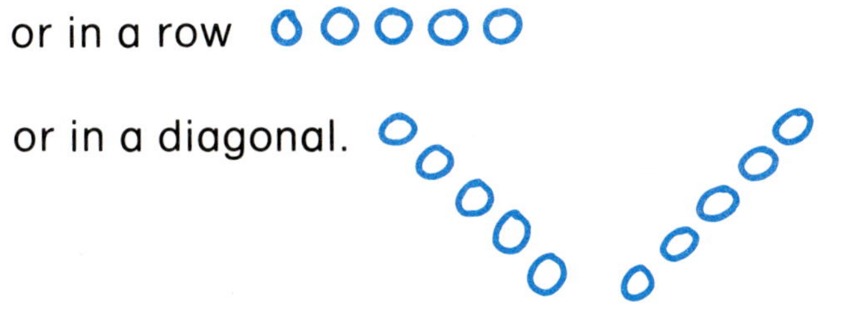

If you want to make it more difficult, use the rule that the five numbers must be **next to each other**.

Using a new square each time, play the game two or three times.
Work out the best way to help you win.

Back to brackets

Remember: Brackets tell us which parts of a calculation belong together. We always work out the part **inside** the brackets first.

Example: $(3 \times 5) + 4 = 15 + 4 = 19$
$3 \times (5 + 4) = 3 \times 9 = 27$

1 Copy and complete these.

a $(5 \times 3) - 2 = \square$
b $5 \times (3 - 2) = \square$
c $(8 \times 6) - 2 = \square$
d $8 \times (6 - 2) = \square$

2 In each of these one pair of brackets is missing. Copy them and put the brackets in the right place to give these answers.

a $6 \times 5 - 3 = 27$
b $8 + 9 \times 2 = 26$
c $18 - 12 \div 3 = 2$
d $20 \div 2 \times 5 = 50$
e $16 + 24 \div 8 = 5$
f $12 + 2 \times 3 - 4 = 14$
g $56 - 28 \div 7 + 9 = 61$
h $18 \div 3 + 6 \times 3 = 36$
i $15 + 5 \times 5 = 100$
j $50 + 45 \div 5 - 4 = 55$

3 Write five number problems which each give 6 as the answer.
You can use: the numbers 1, 2, 3 and 4,
as many pairs of brackets as you like,
any of the signs $+$, $-$, $\times$ and $\div$.

Example: $(3 \times 4) - (3 - 2) - (2 + 3) = 6$

Puzzler

Remember: A product is the number you get when you multiply one number by another.

Today is Liz's nineteenth birthday.
The **sum** of the ages of her two brothers is the same as Liz's age.
The **product** of her brothers' ages is the same as their granny's age.
Granny is 78. How old is each brother?

Precision division

Use a calculator if you wish.

15 724 822
78 1002 65
628 1111 888

1 Which of these numbers can be divided by **3** without a remainder?
Record them. Try ten more numbers of your own.
Copy and complete this rule.

Numbers are **exactly divisible by 3** if the sum of the digits is . . .

Hint: Add the digits.
Then, if necessary,
add the new digits.

16 54 82 999 72
1089 216 5857
585855 834

2 Which of these numbers can be divided by **9** without a remainder?
Record them. Try ten more or your own.
Copy and complete this rule.

Numbers are **exactly divisible by 9** if . . .

Hint: Add the digits.
Then, if necessary,
add the new digits.

215 364 612 5422
417 148 724 62598436
72 345 8016

3 Which of these numbers can be divided by **4** without a remainder?
Record them. Try ten more of your own.
Copy and complete this rule.

Hint: Look at the last two digits
of each number.

Numbers are **exactly divisible by 4** if . . .

Russian multiplication

Here is another way to multiply.

Write a multiplication calculation. For example: 18 × 23

Halve the **left side** and **double** the **right side**. 9 × 46

Halve the left side again (forget about the ½ left over) and double the right side. 4 × 92

And again. 2 × 184

And again, until you get 1 on the left. 1 × 368

Now cross out all the rows which have an **even number** on the **left-hand side**, like this:

~~18 × 23~~
9 × 46
~~4 × 92~~
~~2 × 184~~
1 × 368

Now **add** the numbers which are still on the **right-hand side**.

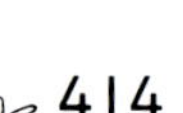

  46
368
___
414

This is the answer to 18 × 23!

1 Use Russian multiplication to work out these.

a 17 × 27
b 22 × 22
c 16 × 125
d 16 × 351
e 25 × 25
f 93 × 6

You can turn the calculations round. Decide which number on the left will give you fewer steps.

2 Why is it not a good idea to use Russian multiplication for:

100 × 652 or 1000 × 831?

Write a sentence to explain.

Doubles and trebles

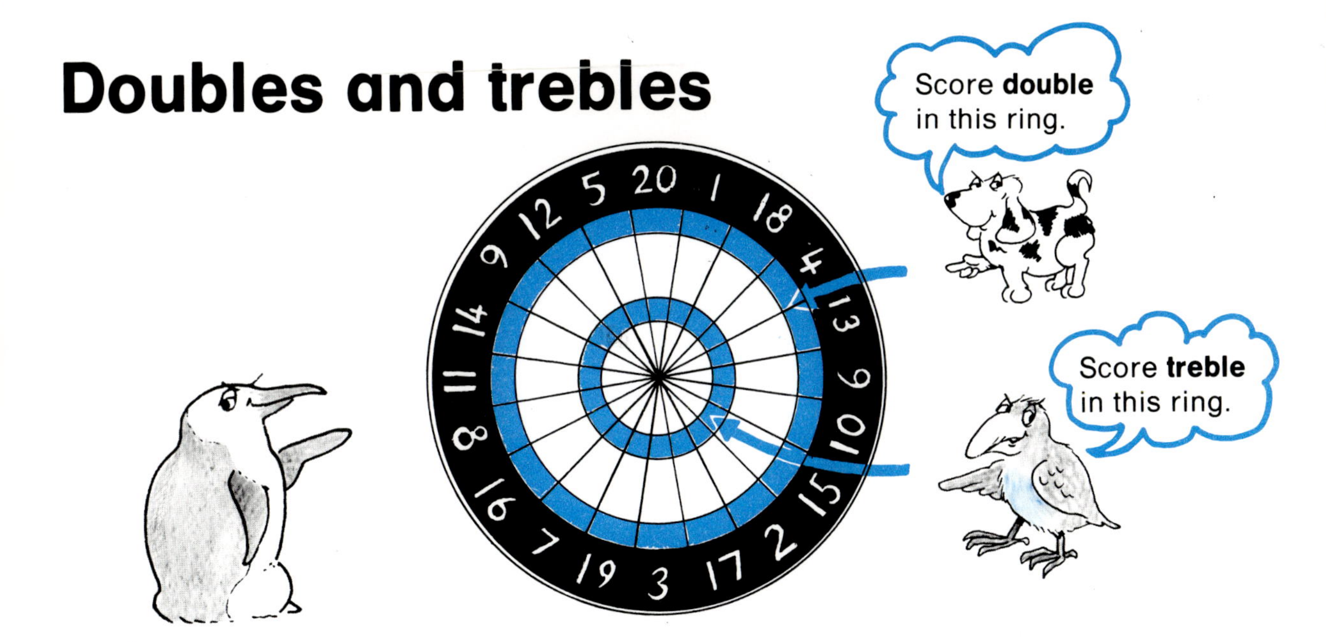

1 List ten ways you can score exactly 36 on this board.
You must use **three** darts. You can **only use the doubles ring**.

2 Now try to score exactly 72 with **three** darts.

a Four ways using **only doubles**.
b Four ways using **only trebles**.

Cross-number

Copy this puzzle on to squared paper.
Make up some clues for the numbers in the puzzle.
They must be multiplication or division calculations or problems.

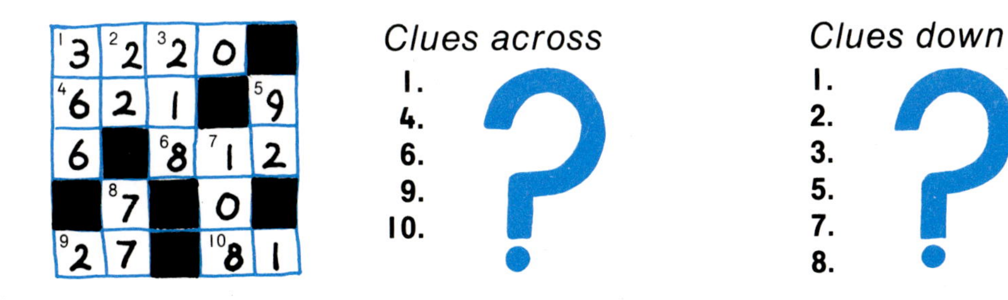

Copy the grid again, leaving out the answers.
Can your friend solve your clues?

Lattice multiplication

Work with a friend. You need squared paper and coloured pencils.
Here is how to use **lattice multiplication** to multiply 52 × 23.

Write the numbers round a lattice and fill in the calculations, like this.

5	2	
5 × 2	2 × 2	2
5 × 3	2 × 3	3

On another lattice, draw diagonals in a different colour and fill in the products.

5	2	
1 / 0	0 / 4	2
1 / 5	0 / 6	3

The tens digit goes in the top of each square, and the units digit goes in the bottom. When there is no tens digit, write in a zero.

Now add the numbers in the lattice. Start at the bottom right-hand corner and add diagonally, like this.

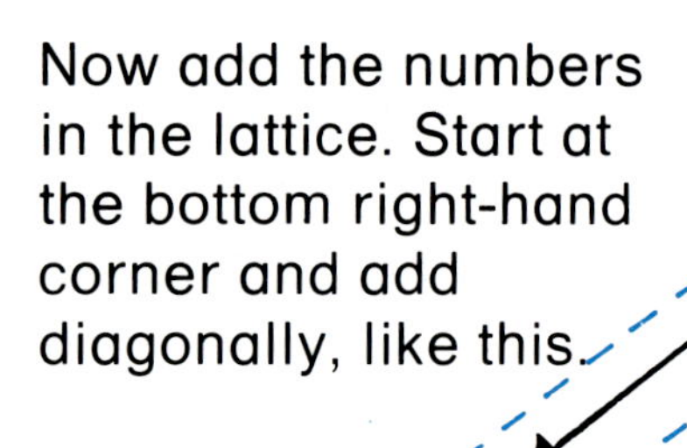

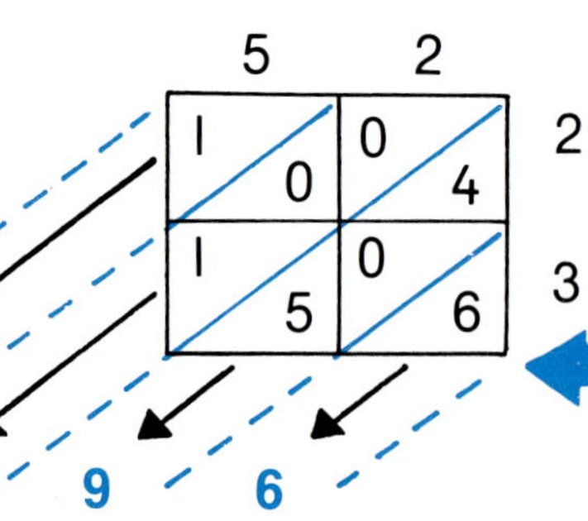

So 52 × 23 = **1196**

Here is how to multiply 47 by 39.

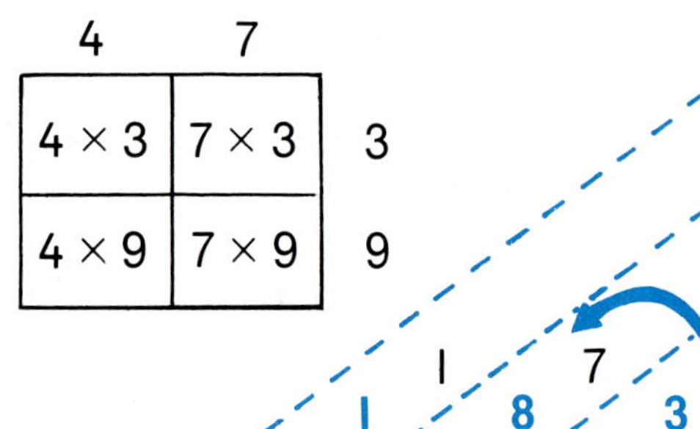

4	7	
4 × 3	7 × 3	3
4 × 9	7 × 9	9

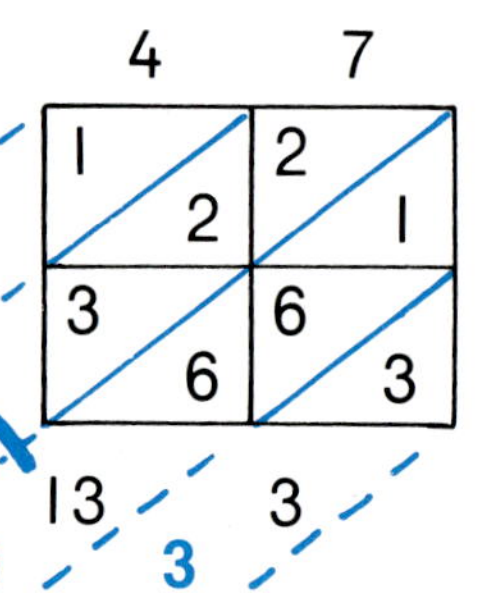

Remember: Carry the one over to the next diagonal to the left.

So 47 × 39 = **1833**

1 Find the answers using lattice multiplication.

a 24 × 37 **b** 34 × 126 **c** 29 × 41
d 88 × 25 **e** 7 × 94 **f** 123 × 456
g 4 × 987 **h** 208 × 107 **i** 2378 × 1654

Check your answers using a calculator.

You will need lattices of different shapes!

2 Write a sentence explaining **how** lattice multiplication works.

Napier's bones

Napier's Bones were invented by John Napier in the seventeenth century. The first ones were actually cut on to bone!

Copy these 'bones' on to squared paper and cut them out. Position them as shown.

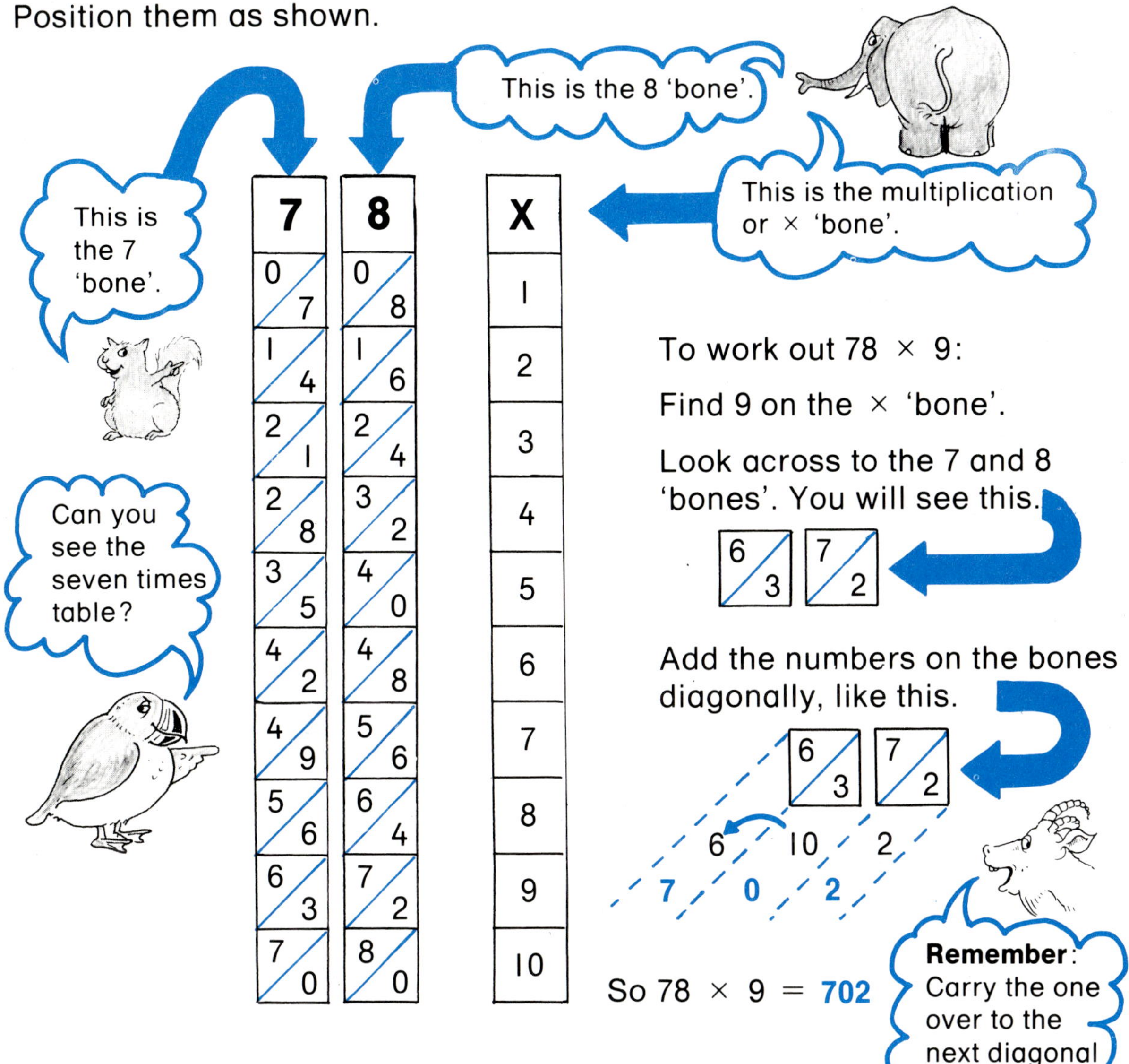

To work out 78 × 9:

Find 9 on the × 'bone'.

Look across to the 7 and 8 'bones'. You will see this.

Add the numbers on the bones diagonally, like this.

So 78 × 9 = **702**

1 Make the 'bones' you need to work out these calculations. Find the answers and write them down.

a 65 × 7 **b** 77 × 7 **c** 98 × 6 **d** 568 × 9 **e** 778 × 3

Check your answers using a calculator.

2 Write a sentence explaining **how** Napier's Bones work.

Four rules!

Work with a friend.

1 Use the number 4 as many times as you like, with any of the signs $+$, $-$, $\times$ and $\div$, to make **all** the numbers up to 20.
Here are some to start you off.

$1 = 4 \div 4$ **or** $\frac{4}{4}$ **or** $(4 + 4) \div (4 + 4)$

$2 = (4 + 4) \div 4$ **or** $(4 \times 4) \div (4 + 4)$

$3 = (4 + 4 + 4) \div 4$

Remember:
You can write
$4 \div 4$ or $\frac{4}{4}$.

2 **Some** of the numbers can be made using **four** 4s only.
Race your friend to see who can find most in ten minutes.

3 Choose another number.
Use it to make the numbers up to 20 in the same way as above.

4 Now make the numbers up to 9.
You can use the figures 1, 2 and 3 **once only** each time.

5 Make up another problem like these for your friend to do.

Eleven divides!

Arrange the digits 4321 in a new order so that the new number can be divided by 11 a whole number of times.

There are eight ways.
Can you find them all?

Using the four rules of number.

Dotty crosses

You need large pieces of dotted paper and coloured pencils.

Mark two crosses and two dots, like this.

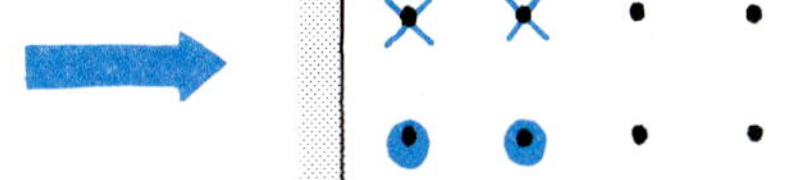

If you join each cross to each dot,
it makes a pattern.
This pattern has **one intersection**.

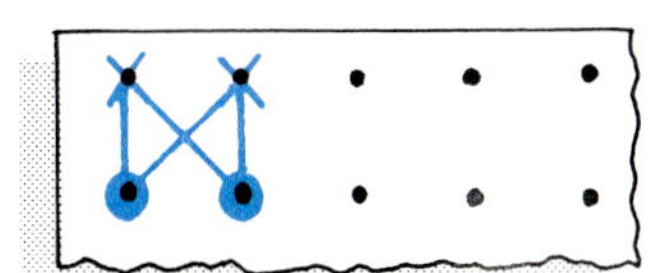

An **intersection** is where two lines cross.

If you mark two crosses and one dot, like this
you get no intersections.

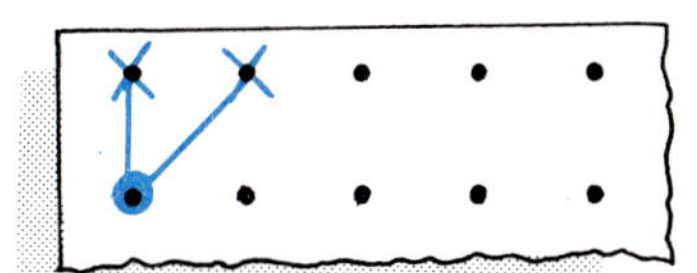

If you mark two crosses and three dots, like this
you get three intersections.

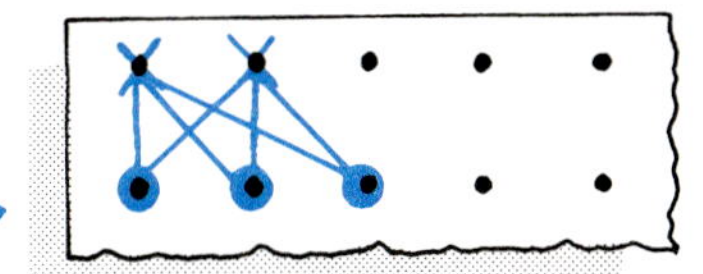

1 Go on like this, using two crosses and **four** then **five** dots.
Write down the number of intersections for
two crosses and all the dots up to five.
Can you find a pattern?

Hint: Count
the intersections
as you make them.

2 Now try with three crosses and one, two, three, four, and
five dots. Write down the number of intersections each time.
Can you find a pattern? Write about it.

Party puzzler

Look at the picture on the front of this book. The yellow boxes
contain novelties (squeakers, trumpets, chicks, hats and crackers).
A teacher buys thirteen of these boxes for a party.
Each child at the party is given three novelties. There are
two novelties left over. How many children were at the party?

Look carefully at the picture and work out
how many novelties are in each box.

Prime numbers

A **prime number** is a number which can be divided only by itself and 1 to give a whole-number answer.
It has no other factors.

Here is a way to find the prime numbers between 2 and 100.
It was first worked out 2000 years ago by a man called Eratosthenes.

You will need a hundred square.

1	2	3	4	5	6	7	8	9	10
11	12	13	14	15	16	17	18	19	20
21	22	23	24	25	26	27	28	29	30
31	32	33	34	35	36	37	38	39	40
41	42	43	44	45	46	47	48	49	50
51	52	53	54	55	56	57	58	59	60
61	62	63	64	65	66	67	68	69	70
71	72	73	74	75	76	77	78	79	80
81	82	83	84	85	86	87	88	89	90
91	92	93	94	95	96	97	98	99	100

Cross out 1. (Mathematicians argue about whether it is a prime number or not!)

Cross out all the **multiples of 2**, except 2 itself.

Cross out all the **multiples of 3**, except 3 itself.

Do the same for the **multiples of 5** and the **multiples of 7**.

1 Using another colour, circle the numbers that are left. Use the rule at the top of the page to see if they are prime numbers. Write them in a list. Call your list *Prime Numbers between 2 and 100*.

2 Write a sentence to explain why you did not have to cross out the numbers which are multiples of 4, 6, 8, 9 and 10.

3 Suppose you wanted to find the prime numbers which are larger than 100. Look at your square to find the next three numbers whose multiples you would cross out. List them in order.

Hint: The third is 17.

Eratosthene's sieve.

More about prime numbers

In the eighteenth century a man named Goldbach had this idea.

Every **even number larger than 4** can be written as the sum of **two odd prime numbers**.

So, think of an **even** number larger than 4.

6

Look at your list of **prime** numbers.
Find two which total 6 when added together.

3 + 3 = 6

Try another.
Think of an **even** number larger than 4.

80

Look at the list of **prime** numbers.
Find two which total 80 when added together.

7 + 73 = 80
or 13 + 67 = 80
or 19 + 61 = 80
or 37 + 43 = 80

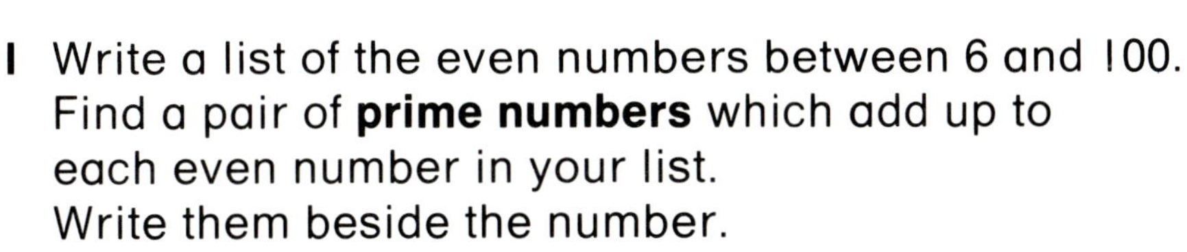

1 Write a list of the even numbers between 6 and 100.
Find a pair of **prime numbers** which add up to each even number in your list.
Write them beside the number.

2 Some of the even numbers have more than one pair.
Write more than one pair for each if you can.

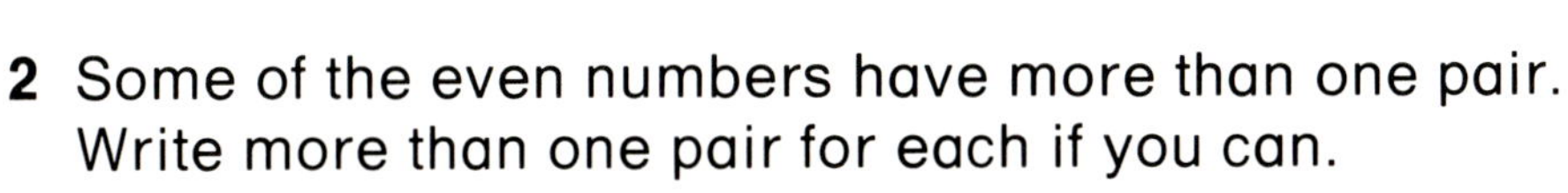

3 100 has six pairs. Can you find them?

4 Why is a **square** number never a **prime** number?

Goldbach's conjecture.

Number power

You may have shown square numbers on a pegboard like this.

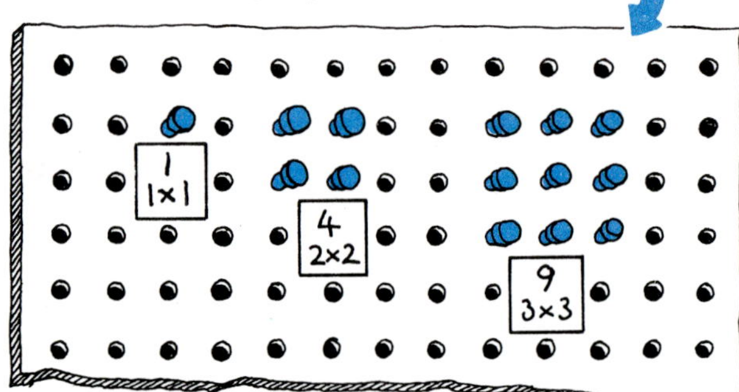

There is a short way of writing square numbers.

	can be written as				
1	⟶	1×1	⟶	1^2	We say 1 to the power of 2 **or** 1 squared.
4	⟶	2×2	⟶	2^2	We say 2 to the power of 2 **or** 2 squared.

1 Copy and complete these.

9 ⟶ □ × □ ⟶ □ We say . . .

16 ⟶ □ × □ ⟶ □ We say . . .

This short way of writing numbers is called **index notation**.

2 Each of these calculations is written using **expanded notation**. Rewrite each one using index notation.

a 5×5 **b** 11×11 **c** 13×13 **d** 49×49

3 These numbers are written using index notation. Rewrite each one using expanded notation.

a 8^2 **b** 12^2 **c** 22^2 **d** 100^2 **e** 63^2

4 Write these square numbers using index notation.

a 16 **b** 49 **c** 144 **d** 100 **e** 64
f 81 **g** 36 **h** 400 **i** 121 **j** 25

Index notation is used to show numbers to other powers.

$8 = 2 \times 2 \times 2 = 2^3$ We say 2 to the power of 3.
$27 = 3 \times 3 \times 3 = 3^3$ We say 3 to the power of 3.
$64 = 4 \times 4 \times 4 = 4^3$ We say 4 to the power of 3.

Did you know that $2^3, 3^3, 4^3, \ldots$ are also called **cubed numbers?**

5 Use index notation to write these.

a $6 \times 6 \times 6$ **c** $24 \times 24 \times 24$
b $19 \times 19 \times 19$ **d** $141 \times 141 \times 141$

6 Write each of these using expanded notation.

a 7^3 **b** 12^3 **c** 37^3 **d** 291^3 **e** 8731^3

7 Expand these numbers and find each answer.
Record like this: $5^4 = 5 \times 5 \times 5 \times 5 = 625$

a 2^4 **b** 2^6 **c** 3^5 **d** 1^7 **e** 10^3

8 Write down the difference between:

a 2 to the power of 6 and
6 to the power of 2.

b 3 to the power of 2 and
2 to the power of 3.

c 4 to the power of 3 and
8 to the power of 2.

9 Find the answers to:

a $9^2 \times 2^2$ **b** $3^2 \times 10^2$ **c** $2^3 \times 5^2$ **d** $1^6 \times 7^2$

10 Now try these:

a $9^2 \div 3^2$ **b** $6^2 \div 2^2$ **c** $10^2 \div 5^2$ **d** $12^2 \div 4^2$

11 List the powers of 2 and 3 like this.

Powers of 2	Powers of 3
$2^1 = 2$	$3^1 = 3$
$2^2 = 4$	$3^2 = 9$

Go as far as you like. You will probably need a calculator.

What is a million?

One million is written as 1 000 000.
It is the same as one thousand lots of one thousand (1000 thousands).
Using index notation, one million is written as 10^6.

1 Use a calculator to work out the following. (The calculator will show numbers after the decimal point. You can leave these out of your answers.)

Remember: There are 24 hours in 1 day and 365 days in 1 year.

a One million seconds make ☐ days.
b One million minutes make ☐ weeks.

2 Do you think anyone could live for:
a one million hours? **b** one million days?

Guess first and then use a calculator to see if you were right.

3 About how long do you think it would take you to count to one million?

Hint: Use a stop-watch to time yourself counting 100.

4 An average primary school has about 200 children. How many schools will be needed for one million children?

5 Your heart beats about 70 times a minute when you are sitting still. How many times would it beat if you sat still for a year? Guess first and then use a calculator to see if you were right.

6 With a friend make some more investigations into

Investigating one million.

On the trillion trail

1 Look up the meaning of these words in several different dictionaries: **a** billion. **b** trillion.
Write down all you can about each one.

2 Use reference books to find:

a the population of your country;
b the population of the world.

Write down these population figures in as many different ways as you can.

Hint: You could use words, numerals, round numbers, expanded notation, index notation, . . .

Super dividends

In a division calculation, the number to be divided is called **the dividend**.

Look at the calculations:

```
  12         6         4
3)36       6)36      9)36
```

9 is 3 + 6,
the sum of the digits
in the dividend.

36 is a **super dividend** because it can be divided a whole number of times:
by **each** of its digits,
and by **the sum** of its digits.

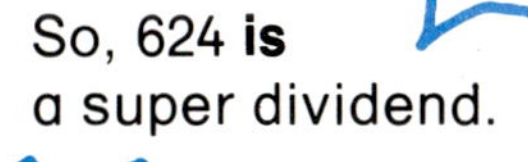

Now let's find out if 624 is a super dividend.

```
  104        312        156         52
6)624      2)624      4)624      12)624
  600                   400          600
  ---                   ---          ---
   24                   224           24
                        200
                        ---
                         24
```

1 Race a friend to see who can find 20 more super dividends in the shortest time. Exchange lists and check each other.

Getting it taped

A hundred square will help you to solve these problems.

1 When I count my collection of cassettes in 5s, I have 4 left over. When I count them in 6s, I have 2 left over. How many do I have?

Hint:
More than 50, less than 90!

2 The total of my collection is a multiple of 7. If I had one more, the total would be a multiple of 5. I have less than 21×4, but more than $28 \div 2$. How many do I have?

3 My collection is smaller.
When I had one less, the total was a square number.
When I buy one more the total will be a cube number.
How many do I have now?

How many more will I need for the total to be both a square and a cube number?

Puzzler

Use each of the numbers 2, 3, 4, 5, 7 and 9 once only.
Which two 3-digit numbers give the largest product when they are multiplied?
Use a calculator if you wish.

Fair shares?

Three pirates, Scarface, Pegleg and One-eye raided a ship. They stole a load of gold bars and took them ashore. They were tired and did not count the bars that night, but decided to share them out equally in the morning.

Scarface did not trust the others. He got up in the night and divided the loot into three equal piles. He buried one pile and hid the bar left over under a coconut tree.

Later Pegleg got up. He divided the remaining loot into three equal piles. He buried one pile and hid the bar left over in a cave.

Later still One-eye got up. He did the same with what was left of the gold.

In the morning they shared the remaining bars equally between them.

WHO GOT WHAT? Work it out and complete this table.

	GOLD BARS			
	buried at night	*hidden*	*received at morning share-out*	*total share*
Scarface				
Pegleg				
One-eye				

When will they meet again?

Seven children like ice-cream.
All seven have bought an ice-cream today.
However, they are very rarely together like this because:

Ali buys an ice-cream **every day**,
Billy buys an ice-cream every **two** days,
Carol buys an ice-cream every **three** days,
David buys an ice-cream every **four** days,
Eve buys an ice-cream every **five** days,
Freddy buys an ice-cream every **six** days,
Gale buys an ice-cream every **seven** days.

How many days from today will they all be buying ice-cream together again?

Hint: You need a *very* long list of the multiples of 7.

A calculator will help you with the list. To count on in 7s, press [7] and [+], then [+] again, and then [=]. Keep on pressing [=] and the display will show the multiples of 7.